# DYNAMIC PRAYER
Prayers That Avail Much
written by
Jothern Robert Smith

Dawn Marie Smith

ISBN: 9781792804236
ISBN-13:

# DEDICATION

We would like to dedicate this prayer manual in memory of a special woman in our Lives, who understood the power of prayer, warfare and deliverance.
Elder Mary C Smith
R.I.H.

# TABLE OF CONTENTS

# ACKNOWLEDGMENTS

We want to acknowledge GOD our Father and the LORD JESUS CHRIST for the assignment he's given us, to make a difference by impacting the lives of others, and through the inspiration of the Holy Spirit. For without GOD none of this would be possible. We want to also acknowledge Apostles David And Wanda Wilkerson, along with TCOR Apostolic and Prophetic Network. For their love, prayers and support of all our kingdom endeavors. Thank you for loving, supporting and encouraging us through the times of turmoil and disappointment, and through seasons of victories, restoration and recovery.

Thank You.

# CHAPTER ONE

# PRAYER OF PRAISE

As we begin the first chapter on praise, we must understand that praise causes us to experience the joyful part of our day with the Lord in prayer and worship even as we wake up in the morning. In *Psalm 92:1, this psalm declares……It's a good thing to give thanks unto the LORD, and sing praises unto thy name, O most high.* Praise is an attitude of expressing our personal gratitude to God. This includes extolling and exalting him just for who he is, and all the marvelous things he has done. There are many ways to praise the Lord and to show how much we appreciate him for all he's done for us. Here are a few words for praise. ***Zamar*** means to touch strings on a musical instrument Psalm 9:2, ***Tehilla*** means a song, hymn of praise Psalm 9:14, ***Halal*** means to boast, to shine, celebrate to make a show Psalm 22:22. The word ***Yadah*** means Extended hands and wringing of the hands in Psalm 28:7, ***Todah*** means sacrifice of praise, thanksgiving, adoration, choir or worshipper in Psalm 100:1, the word **Shabach** means to address in a loud tone, commend, and triumph Psalm 63:3, and **Barak** means to bless God as an act of adoration, to kneel Psalm 145:21. Here in chapter one is just a model prayer of praise. So, let the praise begin.

Heavenly Father, I just want to thank you and praise you today for your mercy endure forever. I praise you for all your many blessings toward me. I praise you with the clapping of my hands, my mouth filled with songs and shouts of praise. I thank you heavenly father for when things are good and through times of turmoil. I will always bless you LORD, that your praise will continually be in my mouth. Heavenly Father I exalt you and glorify your name, for there is none like you for you alone are worthy to receive praise honor and glory. I praise you for you alone are mighty, I praise you for your excellent greatness, I praise you for your mighty acts and with my mouth I will give you joyful praise. All your works shall praise you LORD and your saints shall bless you. In the morning and evening, I will bless you and I will praise your name forever. Great is the LORD and greatly to be praise, your greatness is unsearchable. I will praise your holy name and I will sing unto you a new song in the congregation of the saints, I will praise you with my hands, with my feet and my whole heart I will exalt thee. Heavenly father I will praise you just for your lovingkindness, mercy and truth, for you have magnified you word above your name. As I lift my hands in praise to you, I declare that you are faithful, you are glorious you are perfect in all your ways. I will extol you my king, my God and I will bless your name forever. Oh, how great and mighty are the works of thy hands, blessed be the rock of my salvation and my strength. Great is our God who is mighty in power, full of dominion who reigns forever in majesty. Let the earth rejoice and praise your name. let the angels praise you, let the sun and moon praise you, let the stars and light praise you and let heavens above praise you, let Jerusalem praise you, praise the name of your God for his name is YAH and there is none like him. Let all the earth rejoice, may All the sea creatures and every creepy thing rejoice. Let everything that has breath, Praise the LORD. I LORD shall bless your name forever, for you alone are worthy. My mouth shall offer you praise continually and perpetually. Thanking and praising you O ancient of Days Hallelujah!!!!! Hallelujah!!!! Hallelujah!!!! Glory, Glory, Glory Is the LORD most High who reigns forever and ever AMEN!!!!

# Chapter Two

# PRAYER OF REPENTANCE AND FORGIVENESS

As we enter this chapter, we must know that repentance and forgiveness go hand in hand in our spiritual lives. We must learn to always forgive others, so we may receive forgiveness ourselves from God. Jesus said in *Mark 11:25 And when ye stand praying, forgive, if ye have ought against any: that your Father also which is in heaven may forgive you your trespasses.*

Without repentance we are liable of the judgement from God. With repentance there is a change of a person's mind and turning away from those things that we use to do that we shouldn't do any more. If we withhold forgiveness, then forgiveness will also be withheld from us *Matthew 6:15 But if ye forgive not men their trespasses, neither will your Father forgive your trespasses.* We must strive to be better in this area by allowing the Spirit to convict us of our sins and to forgive others that sin against us as well. Did you know that certain infirmities in our body are the result of not forgiving those in your past relationships? It can also be the result of cultural backgrounds, marriage, social connections through friendship or even forgiving yourself. If this is the case perhaps you can pray this prayer. As you ask the heavenly father to forgive you, also forgive others as well

Heavenly Father as I come boldly to the throne of grace where I may obtain mercy and find grace to help in time of need. I repent right now of all my sins, iniquity and transgressions. Heavenly Father I repent for going places that I should not have gone, things I should not have said that may have offended others. I ask dear heavenly father that you wash me thoroughly from mine iniquity and my tongue from speaking guile. Wash me with hyssop make me white as snow. I ask you GOD to forgive me of the thoughts that are suppressed in my unconscious, subconscious and even conscious mind which are unclean and full of violence in your sight. Heavenly father please forgive me for all the negative words that I have spoken, for you said that death and life are in the power of the tongue: and they that love it shall eat the fruit thereof. I ask for forgiveness as I also forgive those that have misused me, hurt me and those that offended me. Father you said but if I do not forgive, neither will your father which is in heaven forgive me of my trespasses according to Mark 11:26. Father you also said through the Apostle Paul to be ye kind one to another, tenderhearted, forgiving one another even as God for Christ's sake hath forgiving me according to Ephesians 4:32, and I thank you for giving me in Jesus name.

# CHAPTER THREE

# PRAYER FOR BREAKING THE SPIRIT OF ANGER

As we deal with this subject and prayer, we must understand how destructive anger is. Anger is so destructive that this feeling can destroy your family, your health, your marriage and even friendships if not checked. Anger is like a fire once it's out of control, can become a wild fire and affect anything that's close in proximity. If the fire of anger doesn't get put out immediately it can cause substantial damage to yourself and others. In *Proverbs 15:18 it states A wrathful man stirreth up strife: but he that is slow to anger appeaseth strife.* Listen my friend anger can lead to bitterness and resentment even after many offences that never get handled properly, it will ruin your marriage, your friendship and family.

In *Matthew 5:25 Jesus said, agree with thine adversary quickly, whiles thou art in the way with him; lest at any time the adversary deliver thee to the judge, and the judge deliver thee to the officer, and thou be cast into prison.* Basically, Jesus was saying to settle things quickly concerning having an aught against your brother. The apostle Paul declared in his epistle writing in *Ephesians 4: 26-27 He writes "Be ye angry, and sin not: let not the sun go down upon your wrath: Neither give place to the devil".* It is foolish to stay angry for years, days or months with a person. There are many people in life still angry for something that took place years ago, whether it was child molestation, a bad divorce, or even betrayal. People go through the emotion of anxiety and anger every time the person that hurt them comes around, why because they never let that suppressed anger go that they held on to for years. The bible says in *Ecclesiastes 7:9 Be not hasty in thy spirit to be angry: for anger resteth in the bosom of fools.* When a person allow anger to sit dormant, whether do to jealousy etc.., it can go from emotional anger to opening themselves to a demonic spirit which will lead them to domestic violence, homicide or even self-inflicted wounds as a result which can lead them to incarceration and mental institution. Today my friend deliverance is available for you by allowing Jesus to help you to let things go that you've held on to for years, so let's pray.

Heavenly Father I come to you in the Name of Jesus asking you to forgive me of my anger for it is written in Proverbs 14:17 He that is soon angry dealeth foolishly: and a man of wicked devices is hated. I ask heavenly father to forgive me for any strife which I have caused or stirred where I allowed myself to become furious, to abound in transgression according to Proverbs 29:22.

Heavenly Father in the Name of Jesus forgive me of any words that proceeded from my mouth to cause my flesh to sin against you, lest you become angry at my voice and destroy the work of my hands according to Ecclesiastes 5:6. Forgive Me Heavenly Father for being hasty in my Spirit to be angry for anger resteth in the bosoms of fools Ecclesiastes 7:9. Forgive me for the times I let the sun go down upon my wrath giving place to the devil according to Ephesians 4:26,27. Forgive me for allowing the devil room in my life to control my thoughts and the emotions even how I feel towards any situations beyond my control. Instead of acting out my feelings through negative behavior, I should have been forgiving and praying and casting my cares upon you.

Heavenly Father in the Name of Jesus I forgive my father, mother, brother and sister in my family as well as those in my church family, who offended me, abandoned, cheated, abused, mishandled me and overlooked me in Jesus name. Forgive me of any thoughts in my heart and mind of anger or jealousy which caused me to behave irrationally and inappropriately with my actions and speech in Jesus name. Father please forgive me for corrupt communication that proceeded out of my mouth and not that which is good and edifying, so it may minister grace unto the hearer according to Ephesians 4:29.

Heavenly Father in the name of Jesus, I repent for allowing bitterness, wrath, anger, clamorous, and evil speaking to proceed from my lips instead of putting it away from me. Father forgive me for speaking self-inflicted curses against myself and spoken curses against my neighbor, my spouse, my children, Pastor, sister or brother in my family and church family In Jesus name. For it is written in Romans 12:14 Bless them which persecute you Bless and curse not. Heavenly Father Luke 6:28 Declares…Bless them that curse you and pray for them which despitefully use you. So heavenly Father in Jesus name I understand my tongue is a fire a world of iniquity which could not be tame it is an unruly evil, full of deadly poison. For how I can bless you and curse men which are made after your similitude, understanding sweet water and bitter cannot come forth out of the same fountain. Holy Spirit forgive me for grieving you with my actions. So, I renounce the Spirit of Anger, wrath and rage in Jesus name. I bind and command the Spirit of anger to leave my mind, body and soul In Jesus name and never return. I close any breaches, doors and hedges in my Life in Jesus name. I renounce and reject any generational curses of anger from my forefathers including violence and murder associated with anger in Jesus Name. I decree through the Spirit of adoption that I'm no longer associated with my natural bloodline, and I receive adoption by Jesus to himself according to the good pleasure of his will which states in to Ephesians 1:5. I no longer receive the spirit of bondage again to fear according to Romans 8:15, but I receive the Spirit of adoption whereby I cry Abba Father. I decree that the peace of God which passeth all understanding keep my heart and mind through Christ Jesus Philippian 4:7. I loose and permit into my mind, body, soul and spirit Love, kindness, long-suffering, mildness, patience, peace, self-control, and self-restraint right now in Jesus name amen.

# CHAPTER FOUR

# PRAYER FOR BREAKING THE SPIRIT OF BONDAGE

Let's deal with this very important area, where many people have difficulty with. There are addictions of all sorts. These addictions can be very harmful to the body which can cause excessive damage to the liver, kidneys, lungs and even the heart. These addictions include: nicotine, beer, liquor, pain killers, narcotics, heroin, LSD, synthetic marijuana, angel dust, ecstasy, cocaine as well as other illegal substances. These substances are extremely dangerous, they don't just alter your state of consciousness but your reality too. It will cause one to be open to the realm of darkness, most begin to start seeing demons hear voices telling them to do the unusual such as committing suicide, homicide or even cannibalism, because its zombie effects. Some even go as far as overdosing and never recovering. Nicotine within cigarette smoking is one of the leading causes of all kinds of cancer and even leukemia. Many people who have nicotine problems, buy patches, gum, and even electronic cigarettes to help them to stop smoking, when all it takes is the willingness to quit and ask Jesus for deliverance from the spirit of Bondage that seems to plague their life. Don't waste another day destroying the temple that God has giving you to live in. Once the temple fails to sustain you in this life, then sickness and death is inevitable. Below a model prayer for repentance and deliverance to help you in the right direction.

Heavenly Father I come to you in the name of Jesus asking you to forgive me of all my sins, iniquities and transgressions. Forgive me for yielding to the work of the flesh, by being stressed and frustrated, causing me to repeat negative habitual patterns of behavior that leads to sin, iniquities and transgression in my life. It is written in *1Corinthians 6:19,20 that my body is the temple of the Holy Ghost which is in me which I have of God and I'm not of my own? For I am brought with a price and I am to glorify you God in my body and in my spirit, which are yours God.*

Heavenly Father because of this I sinned against you and the Holy Spirit which belong to you. Please forgive me God for every cigarette I ever smoked, pornography I ever watched, narcotic pain killer I've abused and alcoholic drink I've tasted and every act of Idolatry and fornication that I've done against my body and against you in Jesus name. I ask heavenly Father to deliver me, detox me, purge me and break the yoke of bondage in my Life in Jesus name. In Jesus name I renounce today and reject the Spirit of

Bondage destroying my life in Jesus name. I command the Spirit of Bondage to release my mind heart and body In Jesus name. I command every cohort of bondage associated any form of addictions and drugs of heroin, cocaine, methadone, narcotics, pornography, gambling to leave and go into outer darkness In Jesus name. Thank You Jesus for delivering me and I right now receive the Spirit of Adoption where I cry Abba Father in Jesus name. Amen

# CHAPTER FIVE

# PRAYER BREAKING THE SPIRIT OF PERVERSION

Perversion is the most destructive behavior a man or woman to be involved in. It can cause marriages to fail, plus women and children to become victims of rape, molestation, sodomy traumatizing them. Most young people between the ages of 9-17 attempt to live out those traumas, desires and fantasies, and as result victimizing others when they eventually get older. Some young boys and girls are engaged within prostitution, adult films, escorting and other venues to abuse to their body. Mostly it's done by getting body tattoos and body piercings. Being involved by doing such things are open doors and gateways to the demonic realm of darkness. The city of Sodom and Gomorrah were destroyed because of sin that was taking place in the land in Genesis 19:1-24. Perversion is the result of rebellion causing one to commit iniquity against the Lord. Iniquity is a gross act of perversity worthy of punishment by death, such as bestiality, effeminate and sodomite behavior. Here is a what the bible states, *Leviticus 20:15 And if a man lie with a beast, he shall surely be put to death: and ye shall slay the beast.* In most religions in the world such as Mesopotamian and Egyptian religions etc.., are acts of perversion and abuse rooted in idolatrous worship. The Apostle Paul declared to the church of Corinth according to his epistle in *1 Corinthians 6:9,10 Know ye not that the unrighteous shall not inherit the kingdom of God? Be not deceived: neither fornicators, nor* **idolaters,** *nor adulterers, nor effeminate, nor abusers of themselves with mankind, nor thieves, nor covetous, nor drunkards, nor revilers, nor extortioners, shall inherit the kingdom of God.* In other words, those that practice such lifestyles have no inheritance in the kingdom. An effeminate definition according to the Strong's concordance means mal-ak-os fig. a catamite, soft fine. According to the vines dictionary an effeminate is a male who practices forms of lewdness. In others words it's a man with feminine qualities that lay with other men or kept for male prostitution. Abusers of themselves with mankind are those who according to the Strong's concordance are sodomites. These are they that defile themselves with mankind by laying with a male as with a female, a homosexual. Here is a passage in scripture *Romans 1:18-32 For the wrath of God is revealed from heaven against all ungodliness and unrighteousness of men, who hold the truth in unrighteousness; Because that which may be known of God is manifest in them; for God hath shewed it unto them. For the invisible things of him from the creation of the world are clearly* *seen, being understood by the things that are made, even his eternal power and Godhead; so that they are without excuse: Because that, when they knew God, they glorified him not as God, neither were thankful; but became vain in their imaginations, and their foolish heart was darkened. Professing themselves to be wise, they became fools, and changed the glory of the uncorruptible God into an image made like to corruptible man, and to birds, and fourfooted beasts, and creeping things. Wherefore God also gave them up to uncleanness through the lusts of their own hearts, to their own bodies between themselves: Who changed the truth of God into a lie and worshipped and served the creature more than the Creator, who is blessed forever. Amen. For this cause God gave them up unto vile affections: for even their women did change the natural use into that which is against nature: And likewise also the men, leaving the natural use of the woman, burned in their lust one toward another; men with men working that which is unseemly, and receiving in themselves that recompence of their error which was meet. And even as they did not like to retain God in their knowledge, God gave them over to a reprobate mind, to do those things which are not convenient; Being filled with all unrighteousness, fornication, wickedness, covetousness, maliciousness; full of envy, murder, debate, deceit, malignity; whisperers, Backbiters, haters of God, despiteful, proud, boasters, inventors of evil things, disobedient to parents, without understanding, covenant breakers, without natural affection, implacable, unmerciful: Who knowing the judgment of God, that they which commit such things are worthy of death, not only do the same, but have pleasure in them that do them.*

The root of these actions is due to the works of the flesh that are gate ways to welcoming unclean spirits in people lives. These giants in our lives today, if not defeated can cause not just major damage to us, but also the lives of others making them become victims. Understand that perversion is a destiny destroyer of men, women, boys and girls of all ages. Fornication and adultery can defile your spirit, releasing ungodly soul-ties with evil spirits through idolatry and sexual immorality with other people naturally. Those who are married that commit infidelity with those other than their spouse can destroy the marriage covenant. Perhaps my friend you or maybe someone you know is a victim of these acts of perversion. I can assure you that your deliverance is available today through Jesus Christ. Here's valid point, deliverance always comes through our ability to be transparent before Jesus even being honest to ourselves. Let's start by praying this prayer...

Heavenly Father I come to you in the name of Jesus asking you to forgive me of all my iniquities and every habitual behavior that I've done. Blot out my sins and deliver me from my secret faults. I repent for every deed I've done to cause my heart, mind, body and soul to be open as gateways for the enemy to use me to commit lewd behavior. I ask heavenly father In Jesus name wash my mind, eyes and spirit from unclean perverted ways. Heavenly Father as I submit to you, I renounce and resist demons of succubus and incubus that have taken advantage of me through (name of the person) _____________ that molested, raped and sodomized me. Heavenly father I forgive him/her for what he/she have done to me. Heavenly father in the name of Jesus I resist and reject the spirit of perversion associated with pornography, fornication, adultery, doctrinal error, false prophecy, incest, profanity, homosexuality and beastiality in Jesus name. I command you in Jesus name to leave my body, soul and spirit now and go into outer darkness. Heavenly father in Jesus name I ask that you cleanse my eyes of adultery, lust and perversion. I receive right now my liberty, freedom, and deliverance in Jesus name, for who the Son set free is free indeed. Heavenly Father I decree that I shall be holy for you are holy, I decree that my body is the temple of the Holy Ghost in Jesus name. Amen

# CHAPTER SIX

# PRAYER FOR BREAKING THE SPIRIT OF DIVINATION

Many forms of divination and witchcraft that most people enjoy today are evil practices that are taught by demons through idolatrous worship. Many of our forefathers that chose to rebel against the Lord have worshipped practically different gods that are rooted in Canaanite, Egyptian, Babylonian, Mesopotamian, Grecian, Roman religions and even Lucifer himself within occult religion. As a result, many generations of family's curses have been initiated with the results of spell casting, psychic prayers, psychic attacks and causing many sicknesses, deaths, torments and even marriage break ups. It's only the power of God that can break the power of the enemy in our lives, but it must be in Jesus name. Many people are involved in erroneous religions to try to exercise demons out of their homes and families without being born again through spiritual regeneration. In the scriptures there was some individuals who tried to cast out evil spirits but were seriously harmed instead. *Acts 19:11-20 And God wrought special miracles by the hands of Paul: So that from his body were brought unto the sick handkerchiefs or aprons, and the diseases departed from them, and the evil spirits went out of them. Then certain of the vagabond Jews, exorcists, took upon them to call over them which had evil spirits the name of the LORD Jesus, saying, we adjure you by Jesus whom Paul preacheth. And there were seven sons of one Sceva, a Jew, and chief of the priests, which did so. And the evil spirit answered and said, Jesus I know, and Paul I know; but who are ye? And the man in whom the evil spirit was leaped on them, and overcame them, and prevailed against them, so that they fled out of that house naked and wounded.*

Those who are living in darkness cannot cast out demons, they have no power or authority to do so. In our society today many would use crystals, white powder, charms or even talismans to ward off evil spirits, when all it does is welcome more diabolical evil cohorts, and cause more open gateways in their lives. Those openings are causing evil spirits to enter our lives to harass us is quite simple. It is through sin, iniquity and transgression against God and his holy commandments. In these modern times, there are so many people engaging or consulting people involved with witchcraft and don't even realize how dangerous it is. The bible says in *Leviticus 19:31 Regard not them that have familiar spirits, neither seek after wizards, to be defiled by them: I am the LORD your God.* Many parents as well as children ignorantly wear or participate in Egyptian magic as well as psychic palm reading, Pokémon cards, Yu-Gi-oh cards along with crystal balls, gypsy tarot card reading, spell casting, Halloween/harvest festivals, yoga, Ouija boards, Santeria including wearing bless beads, MK Ultra, mime, ventriloquism, necromancy, .hypnosis, obeah, voodoo, medium, stregheria Italian witchcraft, Black magic, obeah, water witching and other mysticisms. Due to different cultural backgrounds, many who practice divination whether by foolish inquiry or deliberately, have opened gateways and demonic portals in their homes, communities, and regions. The bible says in *Leviticus 20:6 And the soul that turneth after such as have familiar spirits, and after wizards, to go a whoring after them, I will even set my face against that soul, and will cut him off from among his people.[7] Sanctify yourselves therefore, and be ye holy: for I am the LORD your God.* If you are a person who have practiced or been susceptible to any form of a curse, spell, hex, or even demonic possession, oppression, even depression, because of or practicing divination, then I believe by you reading this chapter you will repent and change so that the chains of divination be broken. The bible declares in *Galatians 5:20-21 Idolatry, witchcraft, hatred, variance, emulations, wrath, strife, seditions, heresies, envyings, murders, drunkenness, reveling, and such like: of the which I tell you before, as I have also told you in time past, that they which do such things shall not inherit the kingdom of God.*

Let's pray this prayer…. Father In the name of Jesus I come before you to ask that you forgive me of all my sins, iniquity and transgressions. I pray today that as I forgive them that hate me and persecute me, you may also have mercy upon me and forgive me. Heavenly Father in the name of Jesus forgive me for opening any areas of my life where Satan have access in my life because of my own ignorance. I pray heavenly father in the name of Jesus that you forgive me for opening doors, gate ways and portals through Egyptian sorcery, white magic, black magic gypsy crystal ball reading, board and card games such as Pokémon, yugi'oh, even mahjong to read and speak spells to open gate ways in the spiritual realm of darkness In Jesus name.

Heavenly Father forgive me for engaging in any form of pagan rituals and practices and any form of idolatry involving sun worship, Easter, Halloween, ancestral worship, winter solstice, Christmas, and Saturnalia in Jesus name. Heavenly Father forgive me for engaging in any monarch programming such as MK ultra and government projects, holographic repatterning, releasing psychic prayers and attacks through negative thinking, and wishing ill will toward my neighbor to cause bodily harm to come to them In Jesus name. I repent of any involvement with wiccan practices and occults, freemasonry, skull and bones, Knights Templar clubs, other secret societies including college sororities and fraternities, making oaths and denouncing you in Jesus name. I Repent of any vanity of self-worship, man-worship and demon worship, black magic, white magic, puppetry, ventriloquism or any form of deception or illusions in Jesus name. Today Heavenly Father Break every chain and fetter in my life now, for I renounce the spirit of divination operating in my Life. Deliver me Jesus from this evil spirit that has been possessing, oppressing and repressing my Life. I disconnect now from any form of divination through my family linage from my forefathers beginning with Adam down to my generation in Jesus name. Heavenly Father your word declares in Romans 5:19 For as by one man's disobedience many were made sinners so by the obedience of one shall many be made righteous, it is also written in Luke 10:19 you give unto me power to tread on serpents and scorpions and over all the power of the enemy and nothing shall by any means hurt me. So, I bind and abolish every evil serpentine spirit, associated with yoga exercise involving the kundalini awakening to spiritual consciousness in Jesus name. I command every unclean spirit to go into outer darkness and I dethrone you now out of my body, soul, mind and my home In Jesus name. I Loose the holiness of God into my life and purity now in Jesus name Amen.

CHAPTER SEVEN

# PRAYER FOR BREAKING THE SPIRIT OF INFIRMITY

Health is very important as it relates to our mobility in our everyday life. Exercise, healthy eating habits along with proper rest is very significant to our health. Most people across the United States and other Continents have unhealthy lifestyles. This include the intake of too much salt, sugar, smoking, drinking and the use of drugs that can be avoided which is the leading causes of diseases within the body. Let's deal with some of these diseases because of unhealthy eating and seasoning intake within the body. Hypertension (high blood pressure), diabetes, cancer, as well as kidney disease. There are other infirmities that people have that are not associated with unhealthy intakes within the body. Many have suffered from chronic infirmities like fibromyalgia, arthritis, fibroids, sickle cell, muscle dystrophy as well as other infirmities. Many if not all infirmities are due to the unhealthy lifestyle like hypertension but can be demonic oppression from the spiritual realm. Here are some scriptures for reference with evil spirits being the cause of people having infirmities

*Luke 7:21 And in that same hour he cured many of their infirmities and plagues, and of evil spirits; and unto many that were blind he gave sight.*

*Luke 13:11-13 And, behold, there was a woman which had a spirit of infirmity eighteen years, and was bowed together, and could in no wise lift up herself. And when Jesus saw her, he called her to him, and said unto her, Woman, thou art loosed from thine infirmity. And he laid his hands on her: and immediately she was made straight, and glorified God*

*John 5:1 After this there was a feast of the Jews; and Jesus went up to Jerusalem. 2Now there is at Jerusalem by the sheep market a pool, which is called in the Hebrew tongue Bethesda, having five porches.³ In these lay a great multitude of impotent folk, of blind, halt, withered, waiting for the moving of the water.⁴ For an angel went down at a certain season into the pool, and troubled the water: whosoever then first after the troubling of the water stepped in was made whole of whatsoever disease he had.*

Now remember all infirmities are not the cause of evil spirits. So, as we read in this portion of scripture, we read that this man didn't have a spirit, but did have an infirmity.

*John 5:5-9 And a certain man was there, which had an infirmity thirty and eight years. When Jesus saw him lie, and knew that he had been now a long time in that case, he saith unto him, wilt thou be made whole? The impotent man answered him, Sir, I have no man, when the water is troubled, to put me into the pool: but while I am coming, another steppeth down before me. Jesus saith unto him, Rise, take up thy bed, and walk. And immediately the man was made whole, and took up his bed, and walked: and on the same day was the sabbath*

As we see Jesus had a powerful healing and deliverance ministry. Just as it was spoken through the prophet Isaiah where Jesus said in

*Matthew 8:17 That it might be fulfilled which was spoken by Esaias the prophet, saying, Himself took our infirmities, and bare our sicknesses.* Here is another passage of scripture that Jesus read in the synagogue from the prophet.

*Isaiah 61:1 The Spirit of the Lord God is upon me; because the Lord hath anointed me to preach good tidings unto the meek; he hath sent me to bind up the brokenhearted, to*

*proclaim liberty to the captives, and the opening of the prison to them that are bound*

My friend Jesus desires to deliver, heal and restore you. And we desire in prayer the same for you as well. John prayed just a brief prayer in his epistle concerning Gaius.

*3 John 1:2 Beloved, I pray that you may prosper in all things and be healthy, even as your soul prospers.* HNV *(Hebrew names version)*

*3 John1:2 Beloved, I wish above all things that thou mayest prosper and be in health, even as thy soul prospereth.* KJV *(Kings James Version)*

The Lord is just a prayer away cry out to him as Bartimaeus did who was blind, who cried out to him saying, "Jesus thou son of David, have mercy on me!" in Mark chapter 10:47. It doesn't matter whether if a person who is born with a disease or living with one Jesus is a healer. Thank God for the doctors and medicine. First call on the name of Jesus activate your faith and believe it shall be established unto you, whether he leads you to the right physician or heal you through his miracle working power that will astonish the doctors just trust and believe God. Now believe and make this prayer your prayer today.

Heavenly Father in the name of Jesus I come boldly before you and ask that you have mercy on me and forgive me of my sins and make me whole. Your word declares according to Isaiah 53:5 that you were wounded for our transgressions, you were bruised for our iniquities; the chastisement of our peace was upon you and with your stripes we are healed. Jesus, I ask that you make me whole spiritually, soulishly and physically. Your word also declares in Matthew 8:17 saying That it might be fulfilled which was spoken by Isaiah the prophet, saying, yourself took our infirmities, and bare our sicknesses. So heavenly father in the name of Jesus you sent your son and he healed all manner of diseases from Leprosy, Seizures, fevers, hemorrhaging in the body as well as infirmities. So Heavenly Father in Jesus name Let your healing miracle power flow through me now In Jesus name. For it is written in Proverbs 18:21 Death and Life is in the power of the tongue and they that Love it shall eat the fruit thereof. So Heavenly Father I speak with my tongue that I shall live in Jesus name. I declare and decree that it established unto me that according to what is written in 3 John 1:2 above all things that I mayest prosper and be in health, even as my soul prosper In Jesus name. Restore health unto me and heal me of my wounds cure me of this infirmity O Lord. I decree healing from hypertension, diabetes, asthma, arthritis and every chronic disease, respiratory disease, blood disorders, muscles disease In Jesus name and command the Spirit of Infirmity to leave my body now and never to return to my body In Jesus name. Amen.

CHAPTER EIGHT

# PRAYER FOR DESTROYING MARRIAGE BREAKING SPIRITS

As we enter the marriage covenant, let's understand what a covenant is. The Merriam-Webster dictionary and thesaurus definition of the word covenant is a *noun* which means: a formal binding agreement. The binding agreement in a covenant of marriage must be between a man and a woman as God originated it to be since the beginning. In the book of beginnings we read in *Genesis 2:21-24 And the LORD God caused a deep sleep to fall upon Adam, and he slept: and he took one of his ribs, and closed up the flesh instead thereof; And the rib, which the LORD God had taken from man, made he a woman, and brought her unto the man. And Adam said, this is now bone of my bones, and flesh of my flesh: she shall be called Woman, because she was taken out of Man. Therefore, shall a man leave his father and his mother, and shall cleave unto his wife: and they shall be one flesh.*

Always remember just as the Serpent tried to destroy

the unity and covenant that Adam and the woman had with God. Satan wants to destroy the union in the marriage covenant today. It's all about divide and conquer with him. If he can get one of the spouses to act individually away from God and the other spouse, he knows it will eventually breed trouble for their marriage as we see here in our next scripture.

*Genesis 3:1-7 Now the serpent was more subtile than any beast of the field which the LORD God had made. And he said unto the woman, Yea, hath God said, Ye shall not eat of every tree of the garden? And the woman said unto the serpent, we may eat of the fruit of the trees of the garden: But of the fruit of the tree which is in the midst of the garden, God hath said, Ye shall not eat of it, neither shall ye touch it, lest ye die. And the serpent said unto the woman, Ye shall not surely die: For God doth know that in the day ye eat thereof, then your eyes shall be opened, and ye shall be as gods, knowing good and evil. And when the woman saw that the tree was good for food, and that it was pleasant to the eyes, and a tree to be desired to make one wise, she took of the fruit thereof, and did eat, and gave also unto her husband with her; and he did eat. And the eyes of them both were opened, and they knew that they were naked; and they sewed fig leaves together and made themselves aprons.*

Whenever spouses act independently of each other without never trying to come to a place of agreement concerning decisions in their relationship, home, finances and even their children, it can leave open doors within their marriage because of strong opinionated arguments and disagreements. Many of these disagreements can become open door ways for the adversary to get in, if not checked before each spouse go to bed. The Apostle Paul declared in *Ephesians 4:26-27 Be ye angry, and sin not: let not the sun go down upon your wrath: Neither give place to the devil.* To many open doors and gateways can lead to more anger, strife, bitterness, and resentment as well as unforgiveness. It's very important to forgive your spouse or your heavenly father won't forgive you. In the gospel, Jesus declares these words in *Matthew 6:15 But if ye forgive not men their trespasses, neither will your Father forgive your trespasses.* The words of Jesus are very important to us all, especially those who are married. Many spouses choose not to forgive the other because many spouses have only deceived themselves into thinking that their perfect and nothing is wrong. There are other times the spouse will point the finger, blaming the other spouse for the damage they done like Adam did, as well as not accepting responsibility like what the woman did. They both didn't except full responsibility for how things turned out. *Genesis 3:9-13 And the LORD God called unto Adam, and said unto him, Where art thou? And he said, I heard thy voice in the garden, and I was afraid, because I was naked; and I hid myself. And he said, who told thee that thou wast naked? Hast thou eaten of the tree, whereof I commanded thee that thou shouldest not eat? And the man said, the woman whom thou gavest to be with me, she gave me of the tree, and I did eat. And the LORD God said unto the woman, what is this that thou hast done? And the woman said, the serpent beguiled me, and I did eat.*

There are other times when the adversary stirs up spouses deceiving their heart into doing things out of an evil imagination just as the serpent did. This even happens through most disagreements between spouses, sadly most husband and wives don't even pick up an evil spirit working between them to divide and conquer. I must share that there are three evil spirits that mostly break up marriages and that is, Asmodai, deceiving spirit and haughty spirit causing one to have a proud look. Pride causes one not to except responsibility for their own actions, making them self- righteous. The demon Asmodai causes spouses commit excessive extra marital behavior to commit adultery, being in lust. The deceiving spirit causes one to lie to their spouse and themselves, fabricate the story and try to look innocent in the counseling session, basically masquerading the true nature of him or her being the cause the problem. To close open doors and gateways to your marriage, start with prayer, talk without arguing, forgiving one another, also renouncing and dethroning these evil spirits and finally walk in unity together. Within this chapter there is a prayer perhaps you both can pray together.

Heavenly Father in Jesus name we come before you concerning our marriage. Repenting of opening any doors in our relationship through any disagreements, contention strife, jealousy, competition, hatred and unforgiveness for one another. We admit that we were wrong in our approach on how we treated each other. Today heavenly father I choose to forgive my spouse for anything he/she had done to me Verbally, Physically and Emotionally in Jesus name. We ask for your forgiveness for the times we let the sun go down upon our wrath according to Ephesians 4: 26 by in doing so we gave place to the devil in our marriage, home, and family In Jesus name.

Heavenly Father in Jesus name we decree today Unity, wholeness, Love, Kindness, Longsuffering, forbearing one another and showing mercy toward one another. We take Authority over every Unclean Spirit, over every fowl bird and evil Spirit, in Jesus name. We renounce and denounce you Asmodai, Haughty spirit and you deceiving Spirit. With this said we command you to leave our marriage right now in Jesus name. We bind every cohort such as pride, arrogant and lying spirit, spirits of anger, rage, rejection in Jesus name. We bind the spirit of perversion and lust, abandonment, loneliness, low-Self Esteem, and spirit of accusations In Jesus name. We command you to go into dry places never to return. We cast out of our marriage and home Asmodai and call upon the name of the Lord to shoot your arrows to wound Asmodai suddenly according to Psalm 64:7 and may the fire of God consume you and destroy you In Jesus name. Heavenly Father we ask that you to seal up every hedge, open doors and gateways in our marriage today and we loose and permit into our marriage Love, purity, holiness, righteousness, unity and marital longevity and decree it to be so in Jesus name.

# CHAPTER NINE

# COVERING PRAYER FOR THE VISIONS IN THE NIGHT

Dreams and vision are very important in life, because it can reveal prophetic events that affect our present time and the future to come. Sometimes dreams can be the way that God will communicate and speak to us concerning things he wants to reveal, whether good or bad. Most dreams and visions consist of what is revealed in the heart, sensual desires, your purpose in life, other times it can reveal what Heaven or Hell is like. Visions and dreams can also reveal end time events, revelations, warnings, judgements as well as impending dangers, famine and trouble in other countries and even problems in most people lives. There are various types of dreams to name a few, these are repetitious dreams, lucid dreams, visitation dreams, along with precognitive dreams, night terrors/nightmares, epic dreams, violent dreams, warning dreams and even Xrated dreams. Most dreams and visions can be literal or symbolic in nature which a need of interpretation is needed. Dreams can be a series of thoughts and emotions during sleep, as well as creation within the imagination and a release from this reality. On the other hand, a vision is a trance or supernatural experience which carries a revelation, open vision or night vision.

Here's are a few dream examples:

1. **A warning dream** -*Judges 7:13-15 When Gideon came, behold, a man was relating a dream to his friend. And he said, "Behold, I had a dream; a loaf of barley bread was tumbling into the camp of Midian, and it came to the tent and struck it so that it fell and turned it upside down so that the tent lay flat." His friend replied, "This is nothing less than the sword of Gideon the son of Joash, a man of Israel; God has given Midian and all the camp into his hand." When Gideon heard the account of the dream and its interpretation, he bowed in worship. He returned to the camp of Israel and said, "Arise, for the LORD has given the camp of Midian into your hands."*

2. **A visitation Dream**- *(1 Ki. 3:5-15) At Gibeon the LORD appeared to Solomon during the night in a dream, and God said, "Ask for whatever you want me to give you." Solomon answered, "You have shown great kindness to your servant, my father David, because he was faithful to you and righteous and upright in heart. You have continued this great*

*kindness to him and have given him a son to sit on his throne this very day. Now, O LORD my God, you have made your servant king in place of my father David. But I am only a little child and do not know how to carry out my duties. Your servant is here among the people you have chosen, a great people, too numerous to count or number. So, give your servant a discerning heart to govern your people and to distinguish between right and wrong. For who is able to govern this great people of yours?" The Lord was pleased that Solomon had asked for this. So, God said to him, "Since you have asked for this and not for long life or wealth for yourself, nor have asked for the death of your enemies but for discernment in administering justice, I will do what you have asked. I will give you a wise and discerning heart, so that there will never have been anyone like you, nor will there ever be. Moreover, I will give you what you have not asked for—both riches and honor—so that in your lifetime you will have no equal among kings. And if you walk in my ways and obey my statutes and commands as David your father did, I will give you a long life." Then Solomon awoke—and he realized it had been a dream*

Here's a tip whenever you dream make sure you keep a note pad by your bed side, so you can mark down about your dream and ask the Lord for the interpretation. Sometimes if you don't understand then perhaps you need someone who God can use to interpret it. Below is a prayer and petition to God before going to sleep at night, so demonic spirits won't have free course to attack you in the dream realm. Pray that God will speak to you concerning your purpose and his will for your life. If you are an intercessor and your reading this chapter, as God reveal to you through dreams judgements, warning and impending dangers continue to intercede and make up the hedge as a watchman on the wall. Heavenly father in Jesus Name as I come before you I pray that you may reveal to me your secrets in the visions of the night Job 4:13. May you speak to me as you spoke unto Jacob known as Israel in the visions of the night Gen 46:2. Heavenly Father in Jesus name may your visions be clear unto me with the interpretation there of and to know the mystery which you may cause me to behold within the visions of the night. Heavenly Father cover me, my mind, soul and spirit in the night as I sleep. Cover me under your shadow Almighty GOD and be my refuge and my fortress as I trust in you. As you cover me Heavenly father, I shall not be afraid for the terror by night according to Psalms 91. Heavenly Father As you cover me when I sleep, I also pray that you give your heavenly angels charge over me and keep me in Jesus name according to Psalms 91:11, from any tormenting spirit that Satan may assign to me along with his demonic cohorts in Jesus name. May your heavenly angels keep charge over me against demons that may cause me to have night terrors along with night sweats., nightmares and pornographic and seducing dreams during my sleep status in Jesus name.

Heavenly Father I pray as my body temperature become cool at night, I pray no evil shall befall me nor any plague come nigh my dwelling of respiratory sickness such as cold & flu or any such thing come my dwelling in Jesus name. Heavenly Father may you assign Angels with flaming swords to destroy any demons associated with Sleep Paralysis assign to assassinate me during sleep with the evidence of choking, muzzling to try to stop me from breathing as well as trying to snatch my spirit out of my body in Jesus name. I pray that angles with flaming swords would be assign to me, around my home and my bedroom in Jesus name. As you were with Moses and Israel when the lambs blood was applied on the post of the door, so may the Blood of Jesus be applied on every door post and window pane in my home, that the death angel may pass over me and not enter in Jesus name. Heavenly Father tonight I decree that any broken hedges and strongholds that are broken down in my Life and home be repaired and fortified in Jesus name, and I pray that my night visions be pure, holy and peaceful in Jesus name. Amen

# CHAPTER TEN

# PRAYER FOR MAKING DECREES AND DECLARATIONS

As we begin in this final chapter, there are a list of daily decree's and declarations to make as your day begin. Before we begin let us understand what the word decree means in the dictionary. According to Merriam-Webster's dictionary, decree literally means an order usually having the force of law: a judicial decree: royal decree. In the United States there is the U.S. Congress that is the legislated branch of the federal government that makes laws for the nation. Within the congress there are two legislated bodies the first is called the U.S. Senate and the other U.S. House of Representatives. Any elected body can propose new laws that is called a bill. These new laws can be introduced to each house where small groups can discuss and makes changes to it, then afterwards vote on. When each body accepts the bill its then passed and presented to the President. When the president considers the bill, if he approves it then he will sign it into law, if not then he can veto it by disapproving it. In some of the cases, if the President doesn't approve it, then congress can override the President veto and the bill can become law. Now the President can pocket the veto after congress adjourn and once, he does, it cannot be overridden A good leader will always hear a petition and consider a thing before making quick decisions and making decrees that will affect the nation and the people in it. In the book of Esther chapter 8 the king granted the queen her petition and made a decree that could not be overridden for her and the Jews after the hanging of Haman. When a decree is written and sealed, it cannot be changed. Now how much more as we are believers and joint heirs with Christ have that right. The scripture declares In *Job 22:27-28 (KJV) Thou shalt make thy prayer unto him, and he shall hear thee, and thou shalt pay thy vows. Thou shalt also decree a thing, and it shall be established unto thee: and the light shall shine upon thy ways.* In the bible binding and loosing are very important terms to a believer. In other words, to bind is to not disallow, to loose is to permit or allow in the earth as it is in heaven. Remember we are seated in heavenly places with Christ Jesus and we represent the kingdom of God in the earth as ambassadors. So below is a list of decrees to make that it may manifest in the earth realm in your life and family.

Heavenly Father I come before you as your child and joint heir with Christ Jesus to overturn and override any hexes, curses and death wishes upon my life that has been decreed by my enemies. I stand and agree as your son/daughter in the kingdom with the scripture that declares in Job 22 where Eliphaz said unto Job in chapter 22 Thou shalt also decree a thing, and it shall be established unto thee: and the light shall shine upon thy ways.

So today Heavenly Father I decree a thing that it shall be established unto me…

> *I Decree that with your stripes I am healed according to Isaiah 53:5*
> *I Decree Above all things that I mayest prosper and be in health, even as my soul prosper according to 3 John 1:2.*
> *I Decree that your peace which passeth all understanding keep my heart and mind through Christ Jesus according to Philippians 4:7*
> *I Decree victory through our Lord Jesus Christ according to 1 Corinthians 15:57*
> *I Decree the Blessings of Deuteronomy 28*

- that I am blessed in the city and blessed in the field.
- that my basket shall be blessed.
- that the Lord shall cause mine enemies that revolt against me to be smitten before my face, that when they come out against me one way will flee seven different ways.

- that the Lord shall command the blessings upon my storehouses.
- that the Lord shall make me plenteous in goods, and in the fruit of my body.
- that the Lord shall open unto me his good treasure.
- that the Lord shall make me the head, and not the tail, and I shall be above only and not beneath.

*I Decree the windows of Heaven to be opened unto me and pour me out a blessing that there shall not be room enough to receive it according to Malachi 3:10.*

*I Decree that No man should pluck me out of your hand God according to John 10:28.*

*I Decree that No Weapon that is formed against Me shall Prosper according to Isaiah 54:17.*

*I Decree that My days be lengthen according to 1 Kings 3:14.*

*I Decree that I shall spend My days in prosperity and my years in pleasures according to Job 36:11.*

*I Decree that I am more than a conquer through him that loved me according to Romans 8:37.*

*I Decree that I shall not die, but live to declare the works of the Lord according to Psalms 118:17 In Jesus Name*

# REFERENCES:

WEBSTER'S-MERRIAM DICTIONARY
KING JAMES BIBLE
JAMES STRONG'S EXHAUSTIVE CONCORDANCE OF THE BIBLE